D0098154

OSGOOD ON SPEAKING

OSGOOD ON SPEAKING

How to

Think on Your Feet

Without Falling on Your Face

CHARLES OSGOOD

WILLIAM MORROW AND COMPANY, INC.

NEW YORK

Library of Congress Cataloging-in-Publication Data

Osgood, Charles.
    Osgood on speaking: how to
think on your feet without falling on your face.
    1. Public speaking.   I. Title.
PN4121.0835   1988   808.5'1   87-28244
ISBN 0-688-06713-1

Printed in the United States of America

    2 3 4 5 6 7 8 9 10

BOOK DESIGN BY KATHLEEN CAREY

NOTHING TO FEAR

RELAX

Many of us dread having to speak to an audience more than just about anything else in the world. It is most people's least favorite thing. Even dentists, in order to demonstrate that having your teeth worked on is not the most awful thing in the world, like to cite surveys that give drilling, tooth extraction, and root canal work as only the *next* most dreaded experiences there are. Public speaking is number one.

The reason for this dread, psychologists say, is that we are afraid of making fools of ourselves. This is not *entirely* irrational. It is perfectly possible to make a fool of yourself while giving a speech. Furthermore it is not a private failure. By definition, whatever you make of yourself, you are doing so right out in front of everybody.

The more important the speech, the more you have at stake, the more dreadful the prospect of failure, and the more frightened you become. But stop biting your fingernails!

I am here to tell you that public speaking is not difficult and you'd better do it right, or else. My secret is that public speaking is *easy*—one of the easiest things in the whole world. Not just for me—for *you*! For anybody! All you have to do is get over the mistaken belief that it's difficult and dangerous, sort of like high-wire walking.

Relax. Nobody's going to get hurt. Although I'm basically a shy person (honest!), I've been making speeches and appearing on radio and television for more than thirty years, and I can tell you everything I know about public speaking in the time it takes to read this book. Which is not very long. As you can see, this is a short book.

ANYBODY CAN DO IT

Don't make the mistake of thinking that the world is divided into those who can speak in public and those who can't. It is not a "gift" like musical talent or being able to draw. Anybody who can speak can speak in public. Remember that! You are not being asked to do something you've never done before. It's not like juggling or walking a tightrope. It's just plain talking. You talk all the time. It's easy. All you have to do is be at ease and let your mind and your mouth do what comes naturally.

FEAR

The audience won't throw things, you will find with any luck.
But if they do, do not despair, just be prepared to duck.

"We have nothing to fear but fear itself," said Franklin Delano Roosevelt. He was talking about America, of course, but he could have been talking about public speaking.

The principal enemy of the speechmaker is "blind, unreasoning fear." You know perfectly well that the audience is not going to stone you to death, yet the "fight or flight" instincts are triggered, and we become physiologically better prepared either to kill the audience or to turn and run away as fast as our legs can carry us.

The adrenaline is pumping, and our

mental attitude is that of being attacked by a lion.

The last thing we're able to do under those circumstances is to relax and speak comfortably to our audience.

FDR, whatever his political program, was good for America because he *radiated* confidence. With his toothy smile and jaunty manner, he put his audiences at ease immediately. That is what *you* have to do.

DEER IN THE HEADLIGHTS

Have you ever been driving along a country road at night and come upon a deer frozen in its tracks in the beam of your headlights? The deer is so paralyzed by the light that it cannot move—one way or the other. If you didn't stop or swerve, you'd run it over.

Here's my theory about that.

The deer thinks the headlights are spotlights, and what has it paralyzed is stage fright. It thinks the *worst* has happened: It is onstage and has to give a speech. That's why the eyes stare blankly into the blinding light.

Here's how to cope with stage fright when you are frozen stiff with fear.

Pretend that it's *not* a spotlight. Make yourself feel better by pretending they are headlights—and you're about to be hit by a car!

GIVE ME LIBERTY OR GIVE ME DEATH

Stage fright is quite common when in public we appear.
But remember that the only thing there is to fear is fear.

I remember the first time I had to give a speech. It wasn't even my speech. It was

Patrick Henry's speech, the one he made before the Virginia House of Burgesses, March 23, 1775. The immortal "Give me Liberty or give me Death" speech. It was Henry's words I delivered or attempted to deliver before an audience at Our Lady of Lourdes Grammar School in Baltimore, Maryland. I had memorized the words, so there was no problem in that department. But something strange happened, something that had never happened to me before. I took one look at the auditorium full of people and it was as if somebody had stuffed a ball of cotton in my mouth. My tongue stuck to the roof of my mouth. My lips were dry and wouldn't form the words the way I wanted them to. This was stage fright, pure and simple. Years later I would experience it again as "mike fright," and then "camera fright." It is entirely irrational.

You know perfectly well that nobody's threatening you. But your body is getting a message from some part of your brain that there is terrible danger here! You don't need your tongue, the message says, you don't need your lips, what you need are your legs— to run, to flee, to get out of there in a hurry.

So, there you are with your legs all aquiver, ready to run the hundred-yard dash. Meanwhile those things that you *do* need— your voice, your mouth, your brain—are switched to the "off" position just when you need them most.

There is a switch you can pull to turn all these to the "on" position and to get your legs to settle down and keep you standing there, relaxed and comfortable. The purpose of this book is to show you where that switch is—and how to operate it.

FRONT AND CENTER

The problem with getting up in front of a large group of people is that most of us aren't such extroverts that we enjoy that much attention. At first, that is. But you can get so that you like it, once you learn that you can survive the experience and not embarrass yourself up there. When I first started television reporting for CBS News after years of working exclusively in radio, one of the hardest things to get used to was having people gather around and look at me while I was trying to film a "stand-up" into the camera.

After one of these sessions, I ran into Hughes Rudd, the veteran correspondent. He asked me how things were going, and I told him how awkward I felt doing the stand-ups. "That's what I hate, too," said Hughes. "This is not a bad way to make a living, but sometimes you feel like such a damn fool."

LEADERS AND FOLLOWERS

There are leaders in this world and there are followers. Leaders do better than followers, for the most part. They live in nicer homes, drive better cars, and make more money.

Imagine a leader in your mind. Imagine a follower. What is the leader doing? Ah! Gotcha! The leader is up there talking to a group of people. The follower is out there listening. Public speaking is the definitive difference between leaders and followers. Most followers would like to be leaders but feel that they aren't qualified. One major way in which they feel unqualified is that they don't think of themselves as able or effective public speakers. This is too bad because almost *anybody*, unless afflicted with an incredible speech defect, can *become* an effective public speaker. *Anybody!*

So if you are a follower who would like to *become* a leader, read on!

POWER

One of the things you are going to like about public speaking, once you get used to it, is the sense of power it gives you.

We all crave attention. As children we misbehave and carry on to get attention, even if the attention turns out to be a bit more punishing than we had in mind.

Up there on the rostrum, you are king. You've got the audience, potentially anyone, in the palm of your hand. The better you get at it, the more this sense of control will be there. But you will keep the power only as long as you exercise it. Once you *lose* contact with the audience by becoming preoccupied with yourself, the experience becomes a chore on both sides. All you want is to finish and get out of there—and that's all your audience wants, too. If *you* drift away, they'll drift away. Stay with them and they'll stay with you.

WRITING YOUR SPEECH

BE PREPARED

You don't necessarily have to spend weeks in preparation. But if you think you can just get up there and dazzle everybody by making something up as you go along, you are sadly mistaken.

YOU CAN'T GET OUT OF IT!

Many people faced with a speaking date don't like thinking about it. They don't prepare well because they fantasize that somehow they will not *really* have to give the speech. They hope deep down that the event will be canceled—an earthquake or hurricane will strike, *anything* but the dreaded speech.

Forget it. World War III is not going to break out soon enough to do you any good. You may as well get used to the idea that you are stuck. The trick is not how to get out of it but how to make it easy on yourself!

WORRY VERSUS PREPARATION

Worry should not be confused with preparation. Just because you have been thinking about your speech for a long time and dreading it does not mean that you've been doing anything to get ready for it. In fact, worry is counterproductive.

It works like this. The more prepared you are, the less worried you'll be. The less prepared you are, the more worried you'll be. The more worried you are, the less effective you'll be. The more prepared you are, the more effective you'll be. If you know you're going to be effective, you won't worry. If you don't prepare, you *will* worry.

Worry is bad. Preparation is good. As Tom Lehrer wrote in his "Boy Scouts Marching Song,"

Don't be nervous, don't be flustered, don't be scared . . . *be prepared!*

SEMPER PARATUS

The motto of the United States Coast Guard should be your motto, too.

Never appear at a function where you *might* be asked to say a few words without thinking about what you will say if you *are* asked. Make it a habit to do this so that at all times you are ready. You'll get a reputation as a *great* impromptu speaker!

DON'T READ, TRY TO SOUND SPONTANEOUS

Good results are seldom led to
When people feel they're being read to.

Listening to somebody read a prepared text is about as exciting as attending a congressional hearing on interstate commerce. This is because at congressional hearings on interstate commerce the witnesses almost always read their texts, and while they are doing so, congressmen come and go, write letters, huddle with aides, and do everything but *listen* to what is being read. That's all for the record. Unless you are interested only in the record, do *not* read your statement. *Make* it. If you are speaking, *speak!*

One time (October 1985) I flew out to

Los Angeles with Gene Jankowski, president of the CBS Broadcast Group. We went out in the company plane. (There was a CBS company plane, a Gulfstream Jet in those days.) Jankowski was to receive an award, the Humanitarian Award from the National Conference of Christians and Jews.

The only passengers on the flight were Jankowski; his wife, Sally; and myself. So I knew for a fact that this leader of the mass communications industry had prepared himself. He spent a couple of hours writing the speech he'd give accepting the award.

The next night at the ballroom of the Century Plaza, it was a glittering affair, black tie. There were celebrities everywhere. At the dinner, I sat next to Danny Kaye. Kaye would present the award to Jankowski. I, as emcee, would introduce Kaye.

Danny was recovering from an operation and seemed terribly tired that night. Halfway through the dinner, he excused himself and went up to his room to lie down for a while. Poor guy, I thought. He seems in pretty bad shape.

But in an hour, when I introduced him on stage, out bounded this youthful, energetic figure, full of life and spirit. He won the audience right away just by being Danny Kaye—and then he called on Jankowski. Gene walked up with his speech in his hand and Kaye said to him, "No, Gene, don't read the speech, just tell the folks how you feel." And with that he tried to grab the paper out of Jankowski's hand. Gene held on to the script for dear life, and for a few seconds there was a little tug of war up there. Jankowski won. He read the speech as prepared, and it was fine.

But Danny Kaye, the consummate performer, was only trying to help. He was right. Reading *anything* in that situation is not as good as *talking* to the audience, directly and from the heart. Even if it is not as smooth, it is better.

The moral is, if you're speaking to an audience, *speak* to them, don't read to them. If you're giving a talk—*talk!*

NOTES

Although I'm dead set against scripted speeches, I do think it's a good idea for you to use some notes. The notes will help you *remember* what you wanted to say and will remind you where you are in your speech. But what sort of notes? And how to use them?

Here are some actual notecards that I have used to make a speech. I list the key points I want to cover in the order I want to use them. However I do not write down the actual words I'm going to say—or I'd end up reading them. Occasionally I do write down a poem that I haven't memorized or an anecdote that I don't know very well—just to make sure that I get it right, but I try to keep this to a minimum.

You may find in practicing your speech

that you need more detailed notes or perhaps even fewer than I use. Of course each
speaker should adapt his notes to serve his
particular needs—whatever you feel comfortable with, whatever works for you. Just
remember that the *more* you write down, the
more tempted you'll be to look down at your
notes and *read*—and that's what you want
to avoid.

Do remember to make your notes as easy
as possible to read, though. There's nothing
worse than a speaker who can't make out
his own notes!

ORGANIZE

No matter how long or short your speech is
going to be, you've got to get your ducks in
a row. You don't have to know every single
word and phrase you're going to use in the
speech, but you do have to know how you're

going to open, what major points you want to make, and how you're going to close.

You must make sure that the materials you'll need are right there in your hand in the order that you'll need them. There's nothing worse than being up there fumbling around for a piece of paper while the audience is looking on, getting more embarrassed for you with each passing second.

So before you go on, double-check that you've got what you need and in the right sequence. And right side up. An upside-down piece of paper can make you lose your cool up there. And you don't want that to happen.

CARDS

Get in the habit of carrying a stack of filing cards around with you. They're better than a notebook because you can move them around more easily than pages in a book.

When you get an idea, hear a story, a joke, a thought that you think might work in with your next speech—jot it down. Writing it down will help you remember.

Also, when you're trying to assemble a talk later on, you can shuffle through the cards—and you'll be surprised how often an idea will be adaptable to the situation.

Use those same cards to jot down the basic outline of what you want to say in your speech. That's what you bring up on the platform with you—never a script, remember—just those few cards to refresh your memory and remind yourself with little cues as you go along.

The filing card is the speaker's best friend. After you have used cards for one speech, you can file them (hence the expression *filing cards*), and use them again when needed.

① OUTLINE - MAYFLOWER MOVERS DINNER
    BERMUDA - MARCH 6, 1987

OPEN: THEY TOLD ME AS A NEWSMAN ID MEET
    THE MOVERS AND SHAKERS OF THE WORLD.
    NOW ALL I NEED IS TO MEET THE SHAKERS

    THANK LYNN SMITH
    BERMUDA "EVERYONE HAS TO BE SOMEPLACE!"
    TELL "MAN FROM JAPAN" LIMERICK
    CBS CUTBACKS ETC. AS INTRO TO:
MIDDLE → "EXCELLENCE IN MANAGEMENT
    (CONVENTION TOPIC)

    TODAY'S PREOCCUPATION WITH NUMBERS
    BOTTOM LINE
    RATINGS —

② READ PRETTY FACE POEM
MIDDLE (CONT.) QUANTITY VS QUALITY
    MURROW QUOTE
    FUTURE — LONG RANGE
    TELL DISNEY STORY

CLOSE: "WE LOOK UP AT THE STARRY SKY
    AND WONDER AT THE NIGHT
    AND FEEL SO INSIGNIFICANT
    AS WELL INDEED WE MIGHT
    BUT IF WE LET OUR DREAMS PASS BY
    UNTESTED ON OUR SHELVES
    "THE FAULT, DEAR BRUTUS, LIES
    NOT IN OUR STARS, BUT IN OURSELVES"

WRITING YOUR SPEECH

LIMERICK

THERE ONCE WAS A MAN FROM JAPAN
WHOSE POEMS WOULD RHYME BUT NOT SCAN
WHEN TOLD THIS WAS SO
HE SAID "YES I KNOW
BUT I ALWAYS TRY TO GET AS MANY SYLLABLES
INTO THE LAST LINE OF EACH ONE OF MY
POEMS AS I POSSIBLY CAN."

ANECDOTE

HARRY HIRSCHFIELD USED TO CALL BERNARD BARUCH
ON HIS BIRTHDAY. ON BARUCH'S 95TH—
HIRSCHFIELD ASKED HIM: "DO YOU THINK THERE'S AS MUCH
LOVE IN THE WORLD AS THERE USED TO BE?"
BARUCH ANSWERED: "YES, BUT I THINK A DIFFERENT
BUNCH IS DOING IT!"

So WHEN PEOPLE ASK WHETHER NEWS
BROADCASTING TODAY IS UP TO THE ED MURROW—
WALTER CRONKITE STANDARD— I TELL THEM

"YES BUT I THINK A DIFFERENT BUNCH IS
DOING IT."

WHAT ARE YOU GOING TO SAY?

> *If you know there's a lot you've been want-*
> *ing to say and forgive me for being a nag,*
> *All that wisdom and wit but you* still *can-*
> *not fit fifty pounds in a twenty-pound bag.*

Your audience is going to come away from your speech with some impression of you and with one or two of the main ideas you'll be talking about. One or two. Not ten. Not twenty. You are the one who must decide what the one or two ideas are going to be. If there is too much ground to cover, if you try to put ten pounds of content into a five-pound bag, it's not going to work. What are you trying to say? What do you want the audience to feel, or to think as a result of hearing you? Then concentrate on those things. Forget about everything else. Use only those jokes, anecdotes, and so on, that help you to set up and to make those points.

If you cannot express in a sentence or two what it is you intend to get across, then it is not focused well enough. Your talk is going to be all over the place, and your audience will sit there with your message going in one ear and out the other.

After a Sunday church service attended by Calvin Coolidge, newsmen asked the president what the sermon had been about. "Sin," said Coolidge.

"What did the preacher *say* about it?" they wanted to know.

"He was against it," said Coolidge.

MAKE IT PLAIN

*In choosing words, remember when you
write and when you speak
That little words are often strong and long
ones often weak.*

Alexander Gregg once wrote:

There are three things to aim at in public speaking. First to get into your subject; then to get your subject into
yourself; and lastly to get your subject
into your hearers.

The *subject* is all important. Stick to it. Keep
it simple.

The more complex and involved your
speech is, the more difficult it will be to keep
it straight. Not just for your listeners but for

yourself. If can be argued that the more you try to get *into* a speech, the less effective that speech is going to be. Conversely, the simpler it is, the more likely it will be to do the job.

Jonathan Swift, who was a master of words and of ideas, believed that the more words and ideas one had, the more intelligent one was. But I suspect that Swift was not so "swift" a speaker:

> The common fluency of speech in many men and women is owing to a scarcity of matter and a scarcity of words; for whoever is a master of language and has a mind full of ideas will be apt in speaking to hesitate upon the choice of both; whereas common speakers have only one set of ideas and one set of words to clothe them in and these are always ready at the matter; so people come faster out of a church when it is almost empty than when a crowd is at the door.

But there's something to be learned from it. Don't overcrowd the "church" or it may take a long time to empty it out!

WHAT'S IT FOR?

Vagueness has ruined a lot of good speeches, perhaps you have already sensed it.
You must know without doubt what your speech is about, and whether you're for or against it.

Your speech must not only have a topic, it must have a purpose. You have something to sell. Maybe it's an idea. Maybe you want to encourage the audience or make them angry or light a fire under them or maybe just amuse them. Only you know what your purpose is. But you absolutely must have a purpose. If you don't have one, *get* one. If you don't have a purpose, your speech is going to be as unfocused as if you didn't have a topic.

MARLENE AND MIKHAIL

When Marlene Dietrich sent Mikhail Ba-
ryshnikov to pick up her award from the
Council of Fashion Designers in New York,
the great dancer asked her what she wanted
him to say. She said, "Take the thing, look
at it, thank them, and go." Mikhail said,
"That's it?" and she said, "That's it! They
don't have time to listen anyway."

ENOUGH IS ENOUGH

What is enough and what is too much is
going to depend on the occasion. You must

have a sense of what else is on the program and how badly everybody wants to get out of there. As a general rule you are more in danger of being too long, too loud, too serious, too forceful, or too lighthearted than you are of *not* being long, loud, serious, forceful, or lighthearted enough!

HOW LONG SHOULD MY SPEECH BE?
Long enough but not too long.

HOW LOUD SHOULD I SPEAK?
Loud enough but not too loud.

HOW SERIOUS SHOULD I BE?
Serious enough but not too serious.

HOW FORCEFUL SHOULD I BE?
Forceful enough but not too forceful.

HOW LIGHTHEARTED SHOULD I BE?
Lighthearted enough but not too lighthearted.

THE TWELVE-MINUTE SECRET

The standard length of a vaudeville act was twelve minutes. It was the belief of showmen that *no* act, other than the headliner, could sustain interest for longer than that.

Consider, then, if all those troupers singing and dancing their hearts out, if all those jugglers and magicians, those trained dogs and ponies, couldn't go on for more than twelve minutes without boring the customers, what makes you think *you* can, Sweetie?

A SENSE OF WHERE YOU ARE

People who don't talk to audiences very much naturally think of the occasions when they must do so as *important*. Investing an occasion with "importance" in that sense is dangerous because it may be very important to you but not so important to the audience.

You don't think of that last luncheon you attended as super-important, am I right? But if you had to make a speech at that luncheon, you might have felt otherwise. If there is too much of a gap between the speaker and the audience in their understanding of the *weight* of the occasion, this mismatch will get in the way of good communication. Try to sense the *spirit* of the affair and adjust yourself to it. Communion breakfasts and Rotary Club luncheons, political conventions and business meetings—all have different attitudes and feelings that go with them. If you speak to a Communion breakfast as if it were a political convention, the audience will sense that something is wrong. As Dan Rather says, "Wherever you are . . . *be* there."

In addressing the commencement exercises at the Fordham University Graduate School of Business, I told them,

> You are Masters of Business Administration, M.B.A.'s. This means you have learned the skills that will enable you to go far in this world. I, too, am a Fordham man. I have a Bachelor of Science degree. And my own experience in my career is that a little B.S. can take you a long way, too!

KNOW HOW YOU'RE GOING TO END

> *If you want to inspire a group or a mob, a*
> *jury, a panel, or gang,*
> *Let other folks simper,*
> *Don't end with a whimper,*
> *But wind your speech up with a bang.*

When I write a radio or television piece, I often write the last sentence first. I can always change it later if I want to, but the last thing you say is so important because it is what the audience will most likely remember. Also, in structuring your talk, it is enormously helpful to know where you're headed. What the whole talk is leading up to. It may seem ass-backward, but take my advice, write the end first.

Then you can choose any route you want to get there, but at least you will always know where you are headed. If you don't know where you are going, how are you going to recognize it when you get there?

Knowing how you're going to close makes for a strong close. A strong close is one of the most important parts of your speech!

GETTING THROUGH

Just because you'll be up there talking and the audience will be out there listening, it does not necessarily follow that they are going to get what you will say.

Some studies at American University in Washington, D.C., indicate that an average television viewer digests about one third of the main points in a given television news broadcast. One third! In the game of baseball .333 might be a good batting average, but in the game of communication it does not seem too impressive.

There are various reasons given as explanation for the poor performance, and some of them are lessons that any public speaker can profit from:

1. Do *not* assume that your audience already knows as much or anywhere *near* as much as you do about the subject at hand. Do not use specialized language or refer to specialized knowledge without explanation. Otherwise people will lose you. Or I should say, you will lose them.

2. When you make a major point, give it time to sink in. Pause. Do *not* go on to the next point without letting them know that you have just given them something to think about.

3. Do *not* be afraid to repeat yourself. Since audience attention is never 100 percent, it is helpful to tell them what you're going to tell them, then to tell them, then to tell them what you've told them. What I have just told you is a very important point.

USE PERSONAL EXPERIENCES

Go ahead. Indulge yourself. The reason you are up there talking is that you are supposed to have experienced something the audience has not. Share it with them. Make them feel it as you did. How hot or cold it was. How bright or dark. How frightened you were or sad, or annoyed or baffled. The first-person singular is a powerful tool with which to relate to an audience.

MAKE POSITIVE STATEMENTS

*To get across your good idea the best way
you can play it,
Just think of what you have to say and come
right out and say it.*

There's a tendency, when you get before an audience, to be extra careful, to qualify and moderate everything you say. Instead of saying, "The price of eggs is too high!" you say something like "In comparison with the trading levels of other commodities and with market records of the past, the current prices being charged for eggs seem out of line, according to leading specialists."

Don't be afraid to come right out and *say* something. Be direct and unambiguous. If there is a simpler way of saying what you want to say, say it that way.

ASK QUESTIONS

*Your point can be made so that no one will
miss it
When the question is there but the an-
swer's implicit.*

The so-called rhetorical question is one of
the oldest and most useful of devices for a
speaker. It's a way of involving your listeners, leading them along. "How long must
we put up with such gross negligence on the
part of the administration?" "When will the
American taxpayer finally put his foot down
and say, 'This much and no more'?" "And
who, my friends, do you think will be foot-
ing the bill?" Who? Where? When? How?
Sometimes you'll give them the answers.
Sometimes you'll just leave the question to
hang in the air.

TAKE NAMES

Politicians have learned that names are all-important. Make sure you have the *name* of the person who is introducing you. That way you can thank him or her by name. Even if it's a group of strangers, be sure that you have three or four names that you can refer to as you speak. "As Joe Snodgrass remarked to me just a few months ago . . ." "I just want to add my own congratulations to Betty Boomer, your Woman of the Year . . ." "To Pete Krazowski and other incoming officers, congratulations and best wishes for the coming year . . ." You get the idea.

In other words, be a part of the event at which you're speaking. Act as if you have been following the proceedings with interest. That way, as a courtesy, the group may respond by paying attention to *you*!

50

Speaking of names, find out who's introducing you and make sure he or she has *your* name and affiliation right. I have been introduced as "Charles Osgood of NBC" and "Charles Kuralt of CBS."

The late Dale Carnegie used to say that there is no sound on earth sweeter to anyone than the sound of his own name. Remember that!

BEWARE OF JOKES OR HUMOR

Don't tell jokes. You are (probably) not a comedian, and if you tell a series of set "funny stories," you are almost sure to fail. This does not mean you should avoid humor. In fact you should use humor whenever possible, but it should arise naturally from the context of who you are, where you are, and what you have to say. That is what "wit" is all about.

It's not memorizing a joke from some comedy routine.

In 1962, as program director of radio station WGMS in Washington, D.C., I was invited to attend a series of foreign policy briefings at the State Department.

Secretary of State Dean Rusk reviewed the current global situation and introduced each of the assistant secretaries in charge of various parts of the world. I remember that G. Mennen Williams was in charge of the Africa desk at that time.

Each assistant secretary spoke for an hour or so about the crises then afflicting his particular region.

There were wars, insurrections, coups, and assorted troubles in each case, all of which were spelled out in some detail from the U.S. point of view. Finally, the last speaker was President John F. Kennedy. He had just returned from a vacation in Palm Beach. Deeply tanned and wearing a light tropical suit, he looked more like a movie star than a president.

When Rusk introduced him, President Kennedy took the podium, looked at us all, and smiled.

"I know," he said, "that you have been

listening to Secretary Rusk and his assistants all day, telling you about the difficulties we face all around the world. Well, I am here to report that the situation in Palm Beach is stable!"

He got a big laugh, won everybody over, and then began a serious discussion of how events often control presidents rather than the other way around.

The laugh was important. It got us on "conversational" terms with the president. It warmed us up and made us receptive to the important things he had to say.

But it wasn't forced. It came naturally out of who he was, where he'd been, and what we'd been hearing up to then.

OFFENDING PEOPLE

One of the best pieces of advice I ever heard was from the president of a university, whose secret of success was, "Don't get everybody mad at you at the same time." He was talking about running an organization. But the same principle applies to speech making. If you offend first one segment of your audience, then another, then another, pretty soon they will boo you off the stage and run you out of town. So, no ethnic jokes. No dirty jokes. No stories at the expense of anybody's religion. Of course, if you are going to talk about important subjects, they are likely to be controversial and you might have to say things that certain people in your audience don't want to hear. Go ahead. But do not make it worse by insulting anybody gratuitously.

SMALL WORLD

These days anything you say in public is likely to be noted, not only by the audience in front of you but by other audiences as well.

Don't say anything in Los Angeles that you wouldn't want picked up by a New York newspaper. Don't say anything in the South that would embarrass you in the North. And do not say anything *anywhere* that you wouldn't want your *boss* to hear you say.

Word gets around fast these days, and you can't always tell if one of those microphones up on the podium is attached to a tape recorder or to broadcast equipment.

Say whatever you want—but watch out!

AVOID CLICHÉS

Here are some clichés to avoid:

Do not say, "On my left, your right. . . ."
Do not say, "Please hold your applause."
Do not say, "And last but certainly not least. . . ."

Do not say, "That reminds me of the story."
Do not say, "It's a real pleasure to be here."
Do not say ". . . and his lovely wife."

If you want to, though, you can put a twist on the clichés:

"Please hold your boos and jeers."
"And least but certainly not last . . ."
". . . and her lovely husband."

Everybody out there has been to these things before. They know the expected. Give them a little of the unexpected.

KEEP NUMBERS OUT!

When speakers use a lot of numbers
The audience most always slumbers.

If you have researched your subject well, there will no doubt be some numbers you will want to include in your speech. Don't! Numbers may be fine and dandy in an annual report or a statistical abstract. But I am telling you they are death in a speech. The ear simply cannot take in and absorb numbers in the same way the eye can. I know what you're thinking. You're thinking I'll use audio-visual aids, slides and charts. Maybe that will help, but if you don't have anything on those slides and charts prettier to look at than numbers, you are in a lot of trouble anyway.

If you can't keep numbers out of your speech, at least keep them down. A good rule is to use only those numbers you can keep in your head without reference to notes.

If *you* can't keep the figures in *your* head, how do you expect the audience to digest them and keep them in theirs?

SPEECH WRITERS

If you don't trust yourself to write your own speech, a good speech writer can be worth his or her weight in gold. But make sure that even if the words are somebody else's, the ideas are yours. Meet the speech writer before he puts the words on paper. Tell him what it is you want to say. Give him the main points you want to cover. Spending even fifteen minutes with him will be enormously helpful to the writer in picking up the natural cadences and inflections of your voice. You are not doing the writer a favor. You are doing yourself a favor. And your speech will be better for it.

L B J

When you get somebody else to write your speech for you, you open the door to a whole raft of troubles. You are, in many ways, at the mercy of the writer, especially if you don't look at the speech carefully and make revisions—ahead of time, not during the speech.

This story is told of Lyndon Johnson, before he became president:

LBJ was tough on speech writers, demanding, impossible, some said. One writer had had it up to here and decided to quit. His final speech for Johnson was put into the senator's hands in ample time for him to read it, but the writer knew that LBJ probably would not. As usual, he triple-spaced and put only a few lines on a page to make the reading easier for his boss. The script went along like this:

YOU KNOW, AS I DO, THAT THIS COUN-TRY *MUST* TAKE CARE OF THE

NEEDS OF OUR UNDERPRIVILEGED.

(Turn page.)

YOU KNOW AS I DO THAT INCOME TAXES *MUST* NOT BE RAISED

BECAUSE NOW MORE THAN EVER WE MUST PROVIDE INCENTIVE

FOR INVESTMENT AND JOBS FOR OUR PEOPLE.

(Turn page.)

BUT HOW, YOU ASK, ARE WE TO PRO-
VIDE THE FUNDS WE NEED,

MAINTAIN A BALANCED BUDGET, AND
STILL NOT RAISE TAXES?

LET ME TELL YOU HOW, RIGHT NOW.

(Turn page.)

Okay, smart guy, *you're* on your
own!

GETTING READY

REHEARSING IN THE MIRROR

*Mirror, mirror on the wall, you have a lot
    to teach,
But I'm really disappointed you did not ap-
    plaud my speech.*

Don't. It isn't going to do you any good to
practice your speech by delivering it to
yourself in the mirror. The reason is that you
are supposed to be talking *to* somebody, re-

member? And you are supposed to be react-
ing to the *reactions* you get from the
audience. You are not going to get the nec-
essary reactions from the face in the mirror.
Besides, have you ever noticed what people
do when they look in the mirror?

They kid themselves, that's what they do.
They square themselves away, smile sweetly,
stand up straight, and assume a sappy
expression, which is never what they really
look like in actual life *unless* they're looking
into a mirror. Some speech coaches advo-
cate lots of mirror practice, but I disagree
completely. Besides, if somebody walks in the
room and catches you talking to yourself in
the mirror, you are going to feel mighty silly.

THE JACK HANDLE

You can get yourself into a state thinking
about how the audience is going to receive

your speech. Will they laugh at the jokes? Probably not, you think. They've probably heard them before. Will they understand the points you're making? Probably not. They most likely aren't smart enough, you think to yourself. Will they agree with my side of the issue at hand? No, you figure. They most likely have their bread buttered on the other side. Maybe they won't applaud. Maybe they'll boo, you fear. The closer the speech gets, the more you think along these lines, until by the time you stand up there, you're ready to tell them to go to hell!

It's like the city slicker who gets a flat tire in the country. It is raining. He has a spare and a jack but no jack handle. He sees the lights of a farmhouse in the distance and begins walking toward it. He is thinking that if the farmer is home, he'll see I'm in city clothes and he won't like me. He'll see I'm in a bind and won't lend me his jack handle. Maybe he'll charge me to use it. Maybe he'll make me pay fifty or a hundred dollars just for the privilege of using his jack handle once. The closer he gets to the farmhouse, the angrier he gets. When he knocks on the door, the farmer opens it and sees this drenched figure on the porch.

"Come in, stranger, what can I do for you?" he says.

And the stranger glares at him and says, "You can take your stupid jack handle and shove it!"

SLEEP

Sleep is important in speech making. The night before you make your speech, it is important that you get enough. But too often we are so keyed up the night before we have to make an important speech that we toss and turn, and sleep simply won't come. We try little tricks, such as counting sheep, but nothing seems to work. Here's a suggestion. Instead of pretending that you are a shepherd counting his flock (a pretty ridiculous and unlikely role for most of us), simply pretend that you are in an audience listening to a speech, a long, extremely boring speech. Pretend that you are trying to keep awake but that the speech is so agonizingly dull that your head keeps dropping and it's all you can do to keep from falling right out of your chair. We have all found ourselves in that situation, I believe, more often than we have found ourselves tending sheep. By the way, do stay conscious long enough to take note of what the speaker is doing to produce this potent anesthesia. And when the time comes for *you* to speak, don't put *your* audience to sleep that way. As the late Sam Levenson used to say, it's not hard to be brilliant—just think of something stupid and then do exactly the opposite.

TAILOR-MADE

Politicians learn early in the game, if they are smart, that the way you dress and act and speak for and to an audience depends on who is in the audience and what the setting is.

Following Senator Eugene McCarthy around during the Iowa caucus and Illinois primary in 1972, I watched a master in action. McCarthy could be suave and urbane speaking to audiences in Urbana or Chicago, but when visiting the farm country and talking to the folks at a church social or sitting around in somebody's living room, he would be folksy and earthy. Just the sort of fellow who could relate to the *real* problems of *real* people.

McCarthy was an outsider and one of several Democratic candidates that year, and he won neither the primaries nor the nomination. But you could learn a lot from him on the campaign trail. To illustrate how out of touch the other candidates were, McCarthy told this story to the farmers:

> You know that a pig thinks he's warm if his nose is warm. Sometimes a pig will put his nose in the other pig's behind to keep it warm. Pigs have been found in a circle with their noses up each other's behinds—frozen to death. And that's the Democratic Party today!

FEELING SECURE

If you are worried about some detail of your personal appearance, you are not going to be able to concentrate totally on what you are saying. So it's worth the extra effort ahead of time to get your hair cut, your shoes shined, your suit pressed, and so on. Not because anybody out there really gives a damn but because you'll *feel* more confident. The more confident you are, the more natural you can be.

One time in the late 1950s this point was driven home to me forcefully. I was in the U.S. Army, a specialist 3d class. My job throughout my military career was one other soldiers might find quite amazing. I was the announcer for the U.S. Army Band in Washington, D.C. One day on the anniversary of the Battle of Gettysburg, the band played a concert at Dwight D. Eisenhower High

71

School in Gettysburg, Pennsylvania. En route, some of us had stopped to have a little picnic. It had rained the night before, and my shoes got muddy. The Army blue dress uniform was hung neatly in the car, but the shoes were the same ones I would wear to the concert.

As announcer, I had to march, front and center, to introduce each piece and who was sitting out there in the first row, center aisle seat, but Dwight D. Eisenhower, *President Eisenhower*. He was dressed neatly in a tan suit, and *his* shoes were polished, and I had the terrible feeling that as he sat there, his eyes were glued to one thing—two things actually: my muddy shoes.

President Eisenhower had, of course, been General Eisenhower and must have had enough spit and polish left in him to be offended at the sight of this brazen enlisted man standing up there in dress uniform with shoes that looked as if he'd been in combat in some very muddy part of the world.

Off stage between selections I tried cleaning the mud off the shoes. There was no rag available, so I rubbed the shoes on the back of my trouser leg. That was a mistake!

Throughout the concert, the president kept staring at the shoes, and afterward he went backstage to thank everybody. I felt certain that he would say something about the shoes. But he did not. What a guy! No wonder America liked Ike. But I can't recall what I said that day. All I can remember is the shoes.

WHERE AM I?

This may seem so obvious that it should go without saying, but I'm going to say it anyway. Make sure you are talking to the right group!

Very often speaking appearances are at functions taking place in a hotel or conference center. Such places usually have more than one event going on at a time.

It has been known to happen that a speaker will arrive, go to a cocktail party prior to the dinner, may even chat with attendees and be given a speaker's badge and only at the last minute does he discover that the group he's supposed to be addressing is meeting down the hall!

Meanwhile, the group that was expecting him was about to die of anxiety wondering where the heck their speaker might be.

So when you arrive, check to make sure you've got the right event. Otherwise, you might inadvertently find yourself in the awkward position of declaring yourself for governor.

NERVOUS HABITS

There are situations (at a luncheon or dinner speech, for example) when your audience will get its first impression of you *before* you ever take the podium. They will watch you during the meal and as the preliminary announcements, and so forth, are being made. You should follow what is going on, laugh at the jokes, react to what's said, because some people out there will be watching you, and besides you may be able to use some of the information you get.

USING YOUR EYES AND EARS

If you keep your eyes and ears open, you will see and hear things you can use in your speech.

When I delivered the after-dinner speech at the Seventy-fifth Annual Dinner of the Lansing, Michigan, Chamber of Commerce, I noticed that we were marking the eighty-fifth year of the local chamber. So I could say, "Congratulations on this eighty-fifth anniversary of the Lansing Chamber of Commerce and on the seventy-fifth of these dinners. Apparently, you didn't *eat* anything for ten years." They laughed.

At a dinner in Albany, Georgia, honoring the local "Woman of the Year," I noticed that the award being given out was for the "Woman of the Year for 1986"—although it was already January 1987. So I said, "Congratulations to the Woman of the Year for 1986. Too bad it's already 1987. You're already a has-been!"

They laughed.

TO EAT OR NOT TO EAT

If you are speaking at a dinner, they will be serving you food. The phrase *rubber chicken* describes pretty well what you can expect on the rubber-chicken circuit. Should you eat it? This is entirely up to you. It will not affect in any way your ability to speak. If it makes you feel satisfied and content, by all means eat it. Your own sense of well-being is important. But don't eat it just in order not to offend your hosts. They don't care. If you say you never eat before speaking, they will accept that without question.

But if you eat everything—the bread and butter, the chicken, the mashed potatoes, the peas, and even the pudding with the raspberry sauce—you may feel guilty about it. If you begin your speech feeling guilty, you may *look* guilty, and then you are in trouble.

Also you might get fat and feel unhappy about yourself and that might affect your *next* speech.

ON BEING SOBER

> *It's good to be relaxed so it's okay to have*
> *a drink,*
> *But beware that you don't get much more*
> *relaxed than you may think.*

Some experts would tell you never to im-
bibe any alcohol before you speak publicly.
I disagree. As long as you don't overdo it, a
drink can help calm the jitters and put you
in a better mood. That's important.

Understand, however, that one of your
worst unspoken fears—that you are going to
make a fool of yourself—is a clear and present danger if you drink too much. Do not
test your limit on this occasion. It is far more
embarrassing to be drunk publicly than pri-
vately. My advice is if you don't drink as a
rule, don't drink now. If you do drink so-
cially, then it's okay to drink before your
speech. But never take more than one. I'm
warning you. One can loosen you up and
make you feel comfortable up there. Two . . .
you may get away with it—and you may not.
If you don't, it's just awful.

One . . . then stop.

ON BEING OBSERVANT

You are not in a vacuum. You are in some specific place. Indoors, outdoors, huge, intimate. High ceilings, low. No two situations are exactly the same.

Look around. Understand the *context* in which you'll be speaking. Is it a lunch, a dinner? Were cocktails served first? Was there wine at the meal?

You will take your cue from these things as to how relaxed the audience is.

Notice how it is with them. Are they still eating dessert? Are they bored, tired, preoccupied? Has it been a long, long evening? Is there some problem with the lighting or the sound system, so they won't be able to see or hear you? If you don't consider the people you'll be speaking to, how are you going to connect with them?

You're not.

By noticing and responding to them, you are giving yourself the opportunity to involve them in what you'll be doing.

Is it hot and stuffy in the room? Is the air-conditioning *too* effective?

Keep it all in mind!

GO TO THE BATHROOM

Sometime before you're due to speak,
Don't forget to take a leak.

I said this book would be practical, and by God I meant it!

I've told you that you must be comfortable or you cannot make your audience feel comfortable. And you cannot be comfortable if you need to go to the bathroom!

If you are at a dinner, sitting at the head table, you may be loathe to stand up and walk away because you are on display up there. Everybody will notice. But do it anyway. Don't put yourself in the awful position of standing at the rostrum on one foot while you give your speech, simply because you were too shy to excuse yourself while you had the chance.

Giving a speech while needing to go to the bathroom is no good. It is bad for your kidneys, bad for your bladder, and bad for your speech. It does tend to make your speech *shorter*, which is good. But it gives your presentation a kind of wild impatience that audiences can easily misunderstand. Avoid this.

Ask yourself the question I ask all my kids before we embark on a car trip: "Does anybody need to go to the bathroom?" Or better yet, the injunction: "Everybody go before we start, because I'm not stopping on the highway!"

As you give your speech, you will notice people getting up and going to the bathroom anyway. They should have gone before. So should you!

CONCENTRATION

Just before you go on, whether it's in a broadcasting studio or at a Rotary Club luncheon, you should focus on the job at hand and not allow yourself to be thrown off balance. "Getting your feet" is what coach Lilyan Wilder calls it. Sometimes this requires concentration of heroic proportions. One Sunday night, for example, just as I was about to go on the air on the CBS Television Network, somebody in the control room noticed that there was a hair on my shirt collar and so advised the floor director through his earphones. With only a few seconds to airtime, Tony the floor director got up out of his chair, dutifully reached over the anchor desk, and quickly removed the offending hair. Unfortunately, that particular hair happened to be growing out of my Adam's apple and had been firmly rooted thereto. When it was so suddenly and unceremoniously yanked out, the pain was sharp and immediate. Yet within five seconds I was on the air. "Good evening," I said, trying to look cool and professional and not like a man who had just had a hair pulled from his Adam's apple. Try that some time.

CHECK ENTRANCE AND EXIT

He who traces out the route up to the speaking place
Avoids the all-too-common fate of falling on his face.

Make sure of the route from where you are sitting to the point where you'll be speaking. If there are two podiums, make sure in advance which one you'll be using.

Check to make sure there are no obstacles between where you are and where you have to go. If your approach to the podium is awkward, your talk is getting off to an awkward start. One *sure* way to fall on your face is to actually fall on your face en route to the platform. Also, at the end of your presentation, stand there a moment or two to acknowledge applause—and then go sit down. If you seem lost and someone has to *show* you at that point where to go, it will detract from the otherwise marvelous speech you just gave.

WATCH OUT!

What could happen? Well, one thing that can happen while you're up on the speakers' stand is that you might fall *off* the stand.

One memorable evening, Sergeant Mark Hamilton, my predecessor as announcer for the U.S. Army Band, was beginning a live network broadcast before an audience at the Departmental Auditorium in Washington. He climbed up on the rostrum, smiled at the audience, waited for the cue from the director, and at precisely the right moment, to a flourish of trumpets and a roll of the tympani, Mark announced, "Freedom Sings!" Whereupon he completely disappeared. Dropped right out of sight behind the podium. What had happened was that he was standing on a little box to bring him up to the proper height and the box tipped over at just that moment.

It took several seconds for Sergeant Hamilton to recover and resume his introduction.

The moral is, Watch your step. Falling down or off the podium is not the way to put yourself at ease before your audience. An outstanding expert on this subject is former President Gerald Ford. Mr. Ford's reputation as a klutz may have been good for Chevy Chase's career, but it didn't help Mr. Ford's any.

THE MAIN EVENT

THE KEY TO SUCCESS

The audience is just like you and me, for goodness' sake.
So relax and be yourself, and give the audience a break.

The "key" to success as a public speaker, according to my friend Lilyan Wilder, the speech coach, is to be real. If you try to be what you are not up there on the speaker's rostrum, you will not get away with it in all probability. The situation *magnifies* you. Therefore, if you are being phony, the audience will spot it a mile away.

Lilyan tries to get her pupils to "be private in public." In her book *Professionally Speaking*, she explains that before you can be in touch with your audience, you have to be in touch with yourself. There's a writer's maxim: No tears in the writer, no tears in the reader." The same thing applies to a public speaker. And the same thing that applies to tears, applies to laughter.

If *you* don't think a story is funny, the audience won't laugh at it. If *you* aren't moved by the information you're passing on, the audience won't be moved either.

And, most important, if *you* do not have a clear idea of what you are trying to say, there is no way in the world your audience is going to understand what you are talking about.

GIVE

You want to make this a good experience for your audience. To do that, you have to give of *yourself.*

Get in the spirit of that beforehand. Let's say you're sitting up at the head of the table and the woman on your left is the wife of the outgoing president of the organization. To make polite conversation, she will probably ask you some questions about yourself. You can either give her fast answers and try to keep your mind on the speech you're about to give *or* you can give her your full attention and respond with questions of your own about her, her husband, kids, vacations, and so forth. You can be your normal, pleasant, interested self. *That* is what you should do because your normal, pleasant self is exactly who you want to be when you stand up there to speak.

Remember, you are not a robot, delivering your prepared speech to nobody in particular. You are *engaging* the audience members, one at a time and all together. If you want them to be attentive to you, you must be attentive to them!

THE EXECUTION SYNDROME

The very first television program I ever anchored was the *CBS Evening News* one Saturday night in 1972. I'd been doing local radio for years but had recently moved over to the network—where there were both radio and television shows to do.

I was bad. Very bad. The reason I was so bad is that I was so nervous. I'd never been in that spot before. Never felt the heat of the studio lights; never was "made up" by a makeup artist. And here I was—sitting in Walter Cronkite's chair! So I was uneasy, self-conscious, and bad.

Mike Wallace saw my effort at home and at once volunteered to rescue me. He knew a man in trouble when he saw one.

So, on Monday, Mike and I reviewed a tape of the broadcast together. Even before I said, "Good evening," there was the standard studio shot, and Mike, looking at the tape, observed, "You look as if you're about to be executed."

Of course, that was because I *felt* that way.

"Look," Mike said, "you're there, you're the anchorman—you have to 'own' that chair. Sit in it as if it were yours. That's *your* desk, don't act as if you'd wandered off the street and were violating somebody else's property. *You* are in charge. Act that way."

Easier said than done, but Mike was absolutely right.

You, as a speaker, on the television or in a banquet hall must learn how to make it *your* lectern, *your* room. Do that and you've got it made!

HAVE A GOOD TIME

No matter how serious the subject matter, even if you are delivering a eulogy at a funeral—*never* act as if the job were a chore; or one that you would prefer somebody else were doing. *Act* as if you regarded this as a great opportunity to say something that *needs* saying or that you have *wanted* to tell somebody for a long time.

Act as if there were no place in the world you would rather be at this moment than up there where you are. Too many speakers act as if they were in a police lineup. Remember, the key to all this is to identify with the audience.

If *you* don't enjoy it, they won't.

94

HERE'S HOW IT IS WITH AUDIENCES

*Speakers sometimes overlook the Golden
   Rule, I fear.
They go ahead and give a speech that they
   would hate to hear.*

Like them and they'll like you.
Help them and they'll help you.
Enjoy yourself and they'll enjoy them-
   selves.
Be relaxed and they'll be relaxed.
Lead . . . they'll follow.

BUT

If you hate it, they'll hate it.
If you're uncomfortable, they'll be, too.
If you are bored, they'll go to sleep.

THE GOOD GUY

In the movies, the bad guy is mean, self-centered, uptight, suspicious, often nervous and fidgeting. The good guy is relaxed, friendly, self-confident, open, and helpful to people. As a speaker, to put it in the most simplistic of terms, you want to be the good guy!

If you are relaxed and at ease, the audience will accept you, believe you, and trust you. If you are exhibiting the traits of the bad guy up there, they will dislike you, reject you, and most of all they will not trust or believe you.

So we are not just talking about cosmetics or some superficial trivia here. Your ability to be believed and trusted is important because on that depends the effectiveness of your talk. I have seen perfectly decent, smart, hardworking executives suddenly acting like Snidely Whiplash up on the speakers' platform. Remember—you are *not* Snidely Whiplash. You are Dudley Do-right!

ROOM SIZE

You can speak to many folks at once, once you've got the knack,
But be sure that they can hear you if they're sitting in the back.

One of the most important variables in speech making is the size of the room. If people can't hear what you say, it doesn't matter how well prepared or how well presented your speech is. So, if you have a chance while somebody else is speaking—go to the back of the hall and see how it sounds back there. You may be surprised at what you find out.

In general, the smaller the room and the more intimate the setting, the softer and quieter you can be. The bigger the room, the more you have to speak up. And in a *Really* big room, such as the Grand Ballroom of the Waldorf Astoria or in Yankee Stadium, you must speak slowly because it takes time for the words to bounce around. At a stadium, you have to pause between phrases, to let the echo catch up to you. Echo catch up to you.

PUT YOUR AUDIENCE AT EASE

The way to overcome your own nervousness and awkwardness is to think of your audience as being ill at ease. You are there to help them. The poor things. They are terrified. Talk to them. Say with your voice and your eyes and your gestures that you like them. That you are happy to be in their company. Don't just say, "It is a great plea-sure to be here." In fact, *never* say that! Let them know it simply by how you treat them.

THE AUDIENCE IS NOT YOUR MOTHER

Who are they, those people out there? What do you think of them? Psychologists say that performers with stage fright often subcon-sciously think of audiences as authority fig-ures. They are mixed up in our minds with parents, teachers, bosses, and so on. Audi-ences sit there approving and disapproving, responding and not responding. You want their attention, and when you get it, it doesn't always take the form you want. And al-though you need them and want them to love you, you also feel guilty because you don't feel worthy of their love. You also feel guilty because you know that you haven't been the best son or daughter in the world. But wait a minute! This is crazy! Just remember, the audience is not your mother! Once you really accept that, all the craziness will go away. Unless, of course, your mother *is* in the audience. Then you have a problem.

THE NAKED AUDIENCE

I know of one successful speaker who says he imagines that every single person in his audience is sitting there stark naked.

This neutralizes the terrors to some extent. His theory is that you can't be afraid of somebody who doesn't have any clothes on. I'm not so sure about that.

What I'm reaching for is easy conversation. I wouldn't know what to say to a person who didn't have any clothes on. The only time I think you should imagine your audience is sitting there nude is when you are addressing a nudist-colony convention.

GETTING STARTED

The first few moments of your speech are important because you will be establishing the relationship between yourself and your audience. Smile. Say hello with your eyes and gestures. Acknowledge your introducer with a nod and a thank-you. And then wait. Do not begin to speak to the audience until you have everybody's attention. Wait for that. Insist on that.

By waiting, you confirm that what is about to happen is a two-way street. You are not standing up there for your health. You are there to communicate with people, and the communication cannot begin until a connection has been established.

Don't look angry or impatient as you do

this. Simply signal to the crowd that you are willing to wait until you have their undivided attention, even if it takes all night. It won't take all night. You'll be surprised how quickly they will quiet down once it's clear you won't start until they do.

This has the additional advantage of letting the audience know that you are talking to them. *To* them . . . to *them*. Each member of the audience will quickly get the idea that he is being spoken to and will turn on his brain. This is what you want. All too often the speaker conveys the idea that he is reciting words, going through the motions, not really giving a darn whether anybody out there is listening. In fact many speakers seem to *prefer* not being paid attention to. They'd like to sneak on, do their piece, and get out of there without anybody noticing.

That's ridiculous, but it's true. So . . . if you're going to make a speech, you may as well make it *to* somebody and don't start talking before the guy on the other end picks up the phone.

EVERYBODY HAS GOT TO BE SOMETHING

*They tell you you should be yourself and
this will take you far.
So first you have to figure out just who the
hell you are!*

Be something. Do not stand up there and be
nothing. Let the audience read you.

Are you happy? Be happy. Are you angry? Okay, be angry! Be thoughtful, playful,
worried, amused, contented, discontented—
something!

Do not leave it up to the audience to figure out how you feel. Show them! Tell them!
Be shocked or concerned or delighted or dis-
gusted—but be *something*. Okay?

A TIP FROM STANISLAVSKY

The great Russian teacher and theorist about acting, taught that the best way to project one condition is often to mask the condition and try to project its opposite.

Someone who is drunk talks more slowly and attempts greater precision than somebody sober. The way to seem drunk, then, is to seem to be trying to look sober.

The Stanislavsky "Method" actor does not yawn to convey tiredness. Rather he struggles to stifle the yawn. Same with anger or surprise.

The lesson for a public speaker is that if you are trying to seem relaxed, the very *worst* thing you can do is to yawn, stretch, sit slumped in your chair. What you really project when you do those things is somebody who is masking his real emotions. You will seem *more* nervous, not less. The drunk doesn't fool anybody with his demonstration of how he can walk a straight line. You won't fool anybody either. The trick is *not* to mask your nervousness. The trick is not to *be* nervous. You have to convert that nervous energy into *constructive* energy. The *more* energetically you present yourself and your ideas, the *less* self-conscious and nervous you will seem to your audience.

LIGHTEN UP!

> *If you make it bright and brief, you can inform, delight, enthrall,*
> *But if you say too much, they won't get anything at all.*

Unless you are really trying to stir up a crowd and get them to lynch somebody, stop looking so darn mad and serious!

You can always do better with a light touch than with a sledgehammer.

If you raise your voice and shake your fist and your face turns purple with rage, you will *not* come across as the sweet, reasonable person you know yourself to be. To rant and rave may help you get some anger off your chest and let off some steam, but in the long run you will inspire more confidence and be more accepted as a leader if you convey in your bearing and speech that you are in complete control—not only of the situation but of yourself.

John Kennedy was a master of this. He would turn aside an angry question at a press conference with a smile and an easy wit.

In their famous TV debates of 1960, Kennedy and then–Vice President Richard Nixon, respectively, demonstrated the right and the wrong ways to do it. When asked about Harry Truman's propensity to swear now and then, Nixon made a deadly earnest speech about how he would never use such language because, as he said, "I want mothers to be able to hold their children up and say, 'That man is president of the United States!' " and he should be a model and a good example for youth, never swearing or using bad language. (Later, in the Watergate tapes, it was clear how hypocritical Nixon was on this [expletive deleted] subject.)

What Kennedy answered was that after such a long and distinguished career in public service, Harry Truman was a great and respected American and he, Kennedy, would not dream of trying to get Truman to change his language, but would leave that up to Mrs. Truman.

(There's a story, by the way, about somebody complaining to Bess Truman because her husband used the word *manure* to describe some politician's position. "My dear," said Mrs. Truman, "you have no idea how long it took me to get him to say *manure*.")

IT'S NOT THAT IMPORTANT

Keep in mind that although your speech may mean the sun and the moon to *you*, it's probably not that all-fired important to your audience. To you it may be the rare and long-awaited opportunity to sell yourself and your ideas. To the audience, though, it's just another damn speech. At a convention or sales meeting it may the forty-seventh damn speech they've heard this week. So a built-in danger is that you and your audience will be out of synch. Do *not* assume that everybody out there is hanging on your every word. At national political conventions it is pathetic to see all these speakers, one after the other, who have knocked themselves out preparing for the big opportunity, look out on the vast convention floor only to see people milling around, talking, laughing, paying no attention whatsoever. And the TV cameras are off. Dan Rather is not in the booth. *Nobody* is in the booth. It must be an empty, lonely feeling.

ONE ON ONE

The audience is one person. Even though you are talking to a number of people, you are talking to them one at a time. That is to say, they are *hearing* you one at a time. Therefore you should *not* pitch your voice as if you were a drill sergeant addressing a platoon or a teacher lecturing a class. You should imagine, just as I do when I'm on radio or television, that you are speaking to an audience of one. If I were to visualize the number of people *really* out there looking or listening, it would be very troubling indeed. But you bring it all down to size when you realize that if one person gets what you are trying to say, they all will. If one doesn't, none will.

EYE CONTACT

> *Look right at the audience—the audience is king.*
> *Do not look at the microphone. It cannot see a thing.*

If, in normal dealings with people, you avoid looking at them, you will find conversation rather difficult. People expect to be looked at. It's what we do when we talk. Therefore when talking to a group of people, we must look at them, too. But this may be easier said than done.

There are too many people out there to establish eye contact with. Okay, don't try. Just pick out three friendly faces. One left, one right, one center. It doesn't really mat-

ter the size of your audience. You can re-
duce it to three. By speaking first to one, then
to the other, you take in the whole audience.
Everybody perceives you to be looking in
their direction at least a third of the time.
Nobody feels neglected. Yet you only need
to establish and maintain contact with your
three. If you have an opportunity to study
the audience before you begin your speech,
it's a good idea to select your three ahead of
time. Pick people who seem to be alert, alive,
responsive to what's going on. People who
laugh at the jokes. If you find, during your
speech, that one of your three friends seems
to be falling asleep, you must be doing
something wrong.

FOCUS

> *In any public speech you make, the spot-*
> *light is on you,*
> *But* you *must keep your focus on the folks*
> *you're talking* to.

How should you control your posture, your voice, your gestures or your facial expressions?

A tennis pro once described to me a phenomenon he called paralysis by analysis. Yes, you should be holding the racket a certain way and all that, but if you are *thinking* about your knees and your elbows at the moment you swing at the ball, you may very well miss-hit the thing. Hitting the ball is what it's all about.

And for you, the speech maker, your subject is what it's all about.

If you focus on what you have to say and keep your mind on that, you will automatically bring the gestures, voice, facial expressions, etc., etc., etc., all into play—all at the *service* of making your point.

These things are not something you add to a speech, something separate and apart, but spread on like jelly on your toast. It's *part* of your natural expression. In private, you use voice, expressions, gestures *naturally* to express yourself. Now do the same thing in public and you've got it.

PACING AND COLOR

A speech is like a piece of music. It has a theme that is stated and restated. It has a rhythm, which the speaker and his audience must feel. It has dynamic range—sometimes pianissimo, sometimes fortissimo, usually somewhere in between. A good speaker learns to *vary* the tempo, knows when to speed up and when to slow down. The same thing is true of dynamics: get louder or softer, depending on what it is you are saying. Something will *seem* loud if preceded by a whisper. It will seem soft if preceded by a shout.

You are like a pitcher in baseball; even if you have a good fastball, you can't keep throwing the fastball all the time.

You have a variety of pitches. Use them.

A speech that is paced and colored the

same from beginning to end is a speech that will put people to sleep!

BREATHE

Comedian Robert Klein, in his very funny routine about the Lamaze method of "natural" childbirth, points out that the father's principal role seems to be to remind his wife to breathe. That's funny because it seems absurd to think that anybody should have to be reminded to breathe. But under stress we sometimes forget how to breathe *right*. Don't take big, gulping *deep* breaths or try to breathe *faster* than usual. You'll hyperventilate. Just take nice, easy, rhythmic breaths from your diaphragm. It will help you relax. Nobody watching you should be able to notice that you're doing anything out of the ordinary at all. Every actor, singer, dancer, or public performer of any kind knows that

114

controlled breathing is important. Look at the best basketball players in the NBA. Ever notice what Larry Bird or Magic Johnson does on the foul line just before they take a free throw? You and I can learn something from that.

WHAT SHOULD I DO WITH MY HANDS?

One of the strange things about standing in front of a lot of people is that you can suddenly make a problem out of something as familiar as your own hands. Do you feel funny about your hands during the day? Do you ever wonder, even for a moment, what you should *do* with them? Where you should *put* them? Your hands are there at the end of your arms, as always. Unless you have some particular disfigurement or are *miss-*

ing a hand or something, there is no reason whatsoever to imagine that your audience is paying any attention to your hands.

"Look! His hands are on the ends of his arms!"

No, nobody ever says that. So stop thinking about your hands—*except* for how you can use them the way you *always* use them in normal speech.

People vary enormously in how much and in what ways they use their hands in talking. It has been suggested that if you were to tie an Italian's hands behind his back, he would not be able to talk at all!

Public speakers, like private speakers, develop their own particular ways of using their hands during a speech. Winston Churchill would hold on to the lapels of his jacket. This is an old-fashioned debator's posture, which I do not recommend to you. But Churchill made it work. He looked like—well, Winston Churchill when he did it.

You don't want to look like Winston Churchill. You want to look like you.

Do you feel comfortable with your hands in your pockets? Go ahead, do it.

Do you make little one-handed or two-handed gestures when you talk? Go ahead, do it. But remember that some of your audience is in the back of the room. For them, make the gestures bigger.

Do you make grand oratorical flourishes when you talk in private, waving your arms about wildly? You don't?

Then don't do it in public either. People will think you are a raving maniac. Hitler used to work himself into a lather and wave his arms around—and he *was* a raving maniac!

GIVE 'EM A BREAK

Stand up nice and straight and use a voice that's clear and strong.
In other words, do what your mother told you all along.

The way to be a good speaker is to give the audience a break.

Do you like to sit for a long time listening to somebody ramble on? Then don't ramble on!

Do you like having to strain to make out what a mumbling speaker is saying? Then don't make the audience strain. Speak up. Take the mush out of your mouth, as my mother used to say.

Do you enjoy being yelled at or lectured to by other people? Then don't lecture and don't yell. *Talk* to them.

GIVE 'EM A BREAK, PART TWO

When General P. X. Kelley retired as commandant of the U.S. Marine Corps, there was a ceremony at Fort Myer, honoring him and Army Chief of Staff General John Wickham, Jr., who was also retiring after a long and distinguished military career. It was a muggy June afternoon. Vice President George Bush

118

and Secretary of Defense Caspar Weinberger were there. Both the U.S. Army Band and the U.S. Marine Band played. There was a nineteen-gun salute. General Kelley had written a dandy stem winder of a speech criticizing Congress and the news media, and he meant every word he wrote. However, as temperatures climbed into the nineties, several soldiers on the field in dress uniform collapsed in the heat and humidity. So General Kelley, taking pity on the troops, discarded the text and simply said, "There is no prouder commander than the commandant of the Marine Corps, and I salute you. Carry on." Some who were there swear it was the greatest speech they ever heard.

TIME

You should have a little running clock in mind. Your wristwatch will do as an occasional reference, but *never* let anybody see you looking at the wristwatch while you are making your speech.

But you should always be cognizant of where you are in your speech.

(clockface hand at 12) THE VERY BEGINNING

(clockface hand at 1) FIVE MINUTES IN—Getting down to business.

(clockface hand at 2) This is a twenty-minute talk, and I'M HALFWAY THROUGH.

(clockface hand at 3) FIVE MINUTES TO GO—I'm starting to sum up now.

(clockface hand at 4) THE VERY END—The dazzling finish.

Your pacing and delivery will depend to some extent on where you are in your speech. So keep in mind where you are.

GETTING LOST

One of every speaker's greatest fears is getting lost in the middle of a speech. You're afraid you'll turn a page and the vital piece of paper you need won't be there. You can protect yourself ahead of time by making sure everything is in order.

Don't put your notes on the podium ahead of time. Someone might walk off with them. A previous speaker can easily put your papers in with his, and when you get up, there you will be up the creek without a paddle, so to speak.

Don't have your notes in your hand when you walk to the podium. The audience will be looking to *see* what you have, mainly so that they can get out of there if the speech looks too long. Put the notes in a pocket. And remember *which* pocket.

But what if you do screw up?

Not to worry! You are so loose and easy up there and in such control of yourself that you go right on as if nothing had happened. The audience doesn't know you have a problem. Don't *let* them know. Just go on to the next thing, and maybe the missing paper will turn up in the next minute. You must stay relaxed enough to roll with these little crises when they arise. They do arise for every speaker. Your job is not to be ruffled when they do.

PODIUM LIGHT

One time I was giving a speech in Bermuda. It was a convention of Mayflower Movers agents at the Southampton Princess. I was to speak at the awards dinner.

"Do you need anything?" they asked me.

"Audio-visual aids, any special equipment? Anything like that?"

"Is there a light on the podium?" I inquired. "That's the only thing I want to be sure of, because I'm going to read two or three poems."

"There's a light on the podium, and it'll be on," they said.

That night after dessert was served, the chairman of the company introduced me and I went up to the podium, and guess what? No light.

So, I couldn't see my notes and couldn't read the poems, and did I panic? Yes. But not so that they'd notice.

I vamped a little—told them how I'd been told you meet the movers and shakers in the news business but I'd never met so *many* movers before. Then I *mentioned* the light. I said, "This light up here on the podium isn't working. If anybody knows how to fix it, you could come right up here and do it."

And while I told a story or two, somebody did come up and screwed in a new light bulb. "We're finding out how many Bermudans it takes to screw in a light bulb," I said.

The light went on, the little crisis was over, and it was *not* a disaster because I came out and *shared* the problem with the audience. If I had not and tried to struggle my way through in the dark, the audience would *not* have been aware that anything was wrong except that I'd made a poor presentation.

PERFECTION

Are you worried that you will make a mistake and everybody in the audience will find out you are not perfect?

Relax.

They already know you are not perfect. This should remove a great deal of pressure from your shoulders. How do you know that they already know you are not perfect?

Because your fly is open.

DISTRACTIONS

Be sure the people get to eat
Before you stand up on your feet.
For dishes rattle, this is true,
And that will surely rattle you.

It's important to grab and hold the attention of your audience. But this is hard to do if there is some annoying distraction. In fact it's hard for the speaker to keep his mind on what he's saying, let alone for the audience to do so. It's bad manners for waiters to be serving dessert or clearing the tables while you're up there trying to be heard. But you can't just ignore it and plow on through. If it's there, use it. Make some reference to it. Joke about it. Let the audience know that you're as aware of the distraction as they are.

Once, in Columbus, Ohio, when I was

125

giving a talk to a state broadcasters' group, there was only a thin partition dividing the broadcasters' dinner and a wedding party. The rock-and-roll band playing for the wedding party was so loud and so close to the rostrum where I was speaking that I couldn't hear myself think. After joking about it some, I finally threw up my hands and said, "Well, what the hell, let's just listen to the music!" You have to know when you're beaten.

Another time, in Philadelphia, a bell kept ringing in the middle of my speech. I'd wait for the ringing to stop, kid about it, and go right on. This happened three or four times. Finally, when I finished and sat down, someone came up to the microphone and asked everybody to please file out in an orderly manner, *now!*

In the hotel lobby, fire hoses were strung across the floor and firefighters in full battle dress were rushing about. There was a fire! Nobody had wanted to bother us folks at the banquet or interrupt my speech.

There's such a thing as being *too* polite!

If people are talking at one table while you're making an afterdinner speech—you can ask if they can hear you at that particular table. Get their attention, ask the question again. If they say yes, they can hear you, you say, very sweetly, "Well, good. I can hear you, too!"

LOOKING AT THE CAMERA

Unless you are a news reporter or somebody doing a commercial, there is one word you have to remember about looking into the TV camera, if there happens to be a TV camera around. The word is—*don't*. Don't look at the camera. Don't stare at it, don't sneak little glances at it. Just ignore it. You don't have to find the camera. It will find *you*. This applies whether you are a guest on a studio program or out on the street in a rally or demonstration of some kind. The camera is supposed to be aware of you—but *you* are not supposed to be aware of *it*. Ignore it. Pretend it isn't there. If you *do* look at the

127

camera, or wave at it, or suggest in any way that you know it's there ("Hi, Mom!"), I guarantee that the section with you in it will be edited out!

SPEAK BEFORE YOU THINK

Here's the sort of approach that can ruin your day:
"I don't know what I think, till I hear what I say."

"Logic? Good gracious! What rubbish!" says E. M. Forster's old lady. "How can I tell what I think till I see what I say?"

Once you have learned to put your brain in gear while standing before an audience, you will sometimes find that you are capable of expressing quite valid opinions you didn't realize you had.

This is most likely to happen in a question-and-answer session where you can't be sure what the questions are going to be and therefore cannot prepare the answers. Henry James was given some advice by John Jay Chapman:

> Speak out opinions before you think— and before the other fellow speaks. Thus you will give your mind some chance of forming them in a natural way—unconsciously. Accustom yourself to not knowing what your opinions are until you have blurted them out and thus find out what they are.

EVERY SPEECH IS IMPORTANT

My advice to relax and speak in common conversational language to your audience does *not* mean that you should convey to your hearers that what you are saying is unim-

portant. The most serious and urgent of top-
ics can be discussed in ordinary English. In
fact, in "dressing up" a speech in formal
language, the real importance of what you
are saying can be lost.

Every speech is important. Sorry is the
politician, broadcaster, or business execu-
tive who has tossed off a casual remark in a
speech, figuring that he's a long way from
home and nobody would notice, only to find
himself quoted on the news wires and in the
New York Times or *Washington Post.* Ask
James Watt, the former Interior Secretary,
whose efforts at casual speech making and
impromptu news conferences got him into
hot water again and again. A speech can save
the day for you and your cause, but it can
also leave you with your foot planted firmly
in your mouth.

Sir Walter Raleigh, who talked himself
into wealth and finally lost his head, liter-
ally, wrote,

> According to Solomon, life and death are
> in the power of the tongue and as Eu-
> ripedes truly affirmeth every unbridled
> tongue in the end shall find itself unfor-

tunate; in all that I ever observed I ever found that men's fortunes are oftener made by their tongues than by their virtues and more men's fortunes overthrown thereby also than by their vices.

So, while you are being relaxed and conversational up there on the speaker's rostrum, don't be *too* relaxed or *so* casual that you forget that what you say *can* be used against you. If you have engaged your audience so that they are paying attention, that is splendid.

But remember—*you* have to pay attention, too!

UNACCUSTOMED AS I AM

One of the reasons public speaking is dreaded by a lot of people is that they're indeed unaccustomed to it. As with so many other things, the more of it you do, the easier it gets.

If you will apply some of the ideas I have passed along in the preceding pages, I believe you will begin to find expressing yourself in public not only easy, but even pleasurable as you go along. Once you find out that you have the power to hold and interest audiences, you'll derive much satisfaction from doing it and get better and better at it. We like doing the things we're good at.

What I've tried to tell you is that you can be good at it. It's easy once you get the knack, and the knack is no more difficult to come by than, say, using chopsticks, or tying a bow tie. The mysterious becomes simple once somebody shows you how to do it.

Next time it's your turn to make a presentation at a sales meeting, a Rotary Club luncheon, or the PTA, try my approach and see if it doesn't work for you.

Go to it . . . and knock 'em dead!